Awakening

Neil Creighton

Cyberwit.net
HIG 45 Kaushambi Kunj, Kalindipuram
Allahabad - 211011 (U.P.) India
http://www.cyberwit.net
Tel: +(91) 9415091004 +(91) (532) 2552257
E-mail: info@cyberwit.net

Printed at Repro India Limited.

For Diana.

Acknowledgements

Peacock Journal Awakening, River (The Transcendent Tide), Evening, At Piano, Mother and Child at Piano, Bella

Blue Crane Visitation, Homecoming

Verse-Virtual Recovery, The Eagle, Willy Wagtail, Black Cockatoos, Birds, High Country Rail Trail, North of Somewhere, La Loire a Velo, Blue Mountains Grotto, Morning Light, Is it Not Enough, I Know You are a Gift from God, I am Amongst the Richest of Men, Lament for a Lighthorseman, Can We Not Live Together, It's Not Our Fault, The Gathering Host, Australian Inferno (Summer),

Silver Birch Press Into the Wonder, The Millet Cutters, Summers With Jean, Remember

Nature Writing The Diamond Python, Lyre Birds

Gnarled Oak I woke this morning

One Sentence Poems I Wake, Winter

Poetry Quarterly The Phosphorescence Lapping, Fate

Prosposia Temple

The Second Genesis Wilpena Pound, Earth Music

Whispers in the Wind Island of Songs, Seals at Play, Hush, The Plum Tree

Anti-Heroin Chic At the Victoria and Albert Museum

Praxis Mag Online The Fallen Forest Tree, Elegy for Ikeogu Oke

South Florida Poetry Journal Somme Cemetery

New Verse News Koko and the Beast

Poets Reading the News The Green Sea Turtle

The Bees Are Dead Advertisement

Avocet Spring, Autumn

The Ekphrastic Review Desert Ruin

Guy Farmer's Social Justice Poetry Interim Report

Autumn Sky Daily Then

Contents

Part 1. Gifts the Darkness Brings 9

Awakening 10
I Remember 11
Visitation 13
Recovery 14
I Hear the Music 15
Into the Wonder 17

Part 2. A Weight of Thankfulness 19

The Diamond Python 20
Seals At Play 22
The Eagle 24
Willy Wagtail 25
Lyre Birds 26
Birds 28
i woke this morning 29
I wake 30
The Phosphorescence Lapping 31

Part 3. Music Everywhere Resounds 33

Temple 34
Remember 35
Wilpena Pound 37
High Country Rail Trail 39
North of Somewhere 41
La Loire a Velo 43
At the Victoria & Albert Museum 44
Island of Songs 46
Evening 48

The Fallen Forest Tree 49
Desert Ruin 50
Spring 51
Summer Inferno 52
Autumn Day 55
Winter 56
Home 57

Part 4. Melody Upon Melody **59**

My Flawed Love 60
Earth Music 61
River 63
This Passing Day 65
I know 66
Come, Hold Me 67
Fate 68
The Millet Cutters 72
I Am Amongst the Richest of Men 74
Hush 76
Mother and Child at Piano 77
Bella 78
At Piano 79

Part 5. The Tide Rushes Out **81**

Lament for a Light Horseman 82
Homecoming 85
Summers With Jean 87
Elegy for Ikeogu Oke 89
Somme Cemetery 92
Koko and the Beast 94
The Green Sea Turtle 96
Advertisement 97
Interim Report 99

Can We Not Live Together? 101
Then 103
The Gathering Host 105
It's Not Our Fault 107
The Plum Tree 109

Part 1. Gifts the Darkness Brings

Awakening

Beyond morphine detachment,
out of the bed's encircled darkness,
when pain recedes just enough
to let the mind tiptoe
a cautious step or two,

through a small window
in the antiseptic room
comes a gift the darkness brings,
a rush of revelation,
just glint of light playing on green leaves
swaying to the wind's caress,
sun-dappled tangle of branches,
cloud-flecked blue sky,

but each simple, commonplace moment
transformed, miraculously new,
never truly seen before,
now shouting glory to ears
that had been deaf,
beauty to eyes
that had been blind.

I Remember

I remember
mumbled words,
tumour, cancer, lymph nodes, chemotherapy, sorry,
light touch of hand on my shoulder,
look of sympathy before the door closed.

I remember
her tender words,
We'll get through this together, Neil,
her soft kiss, her gentle touch,
her look of love before she left.

I remember
the endless night's utter despair,
the fierce heat of death's breath,
the sleepless desolation, the repeating questions,
Is this the end? Here? Now? Like this?

I remember
leaving that pain-wracked body,
wounded from chest bone to pubic bone,
looking at it with curious objectivity, thinking
That body on the bed, is it me?

I remember
travelling somewhere, I don't know where,
somewhere utterly dark, a lightless void,
and I remember the voice.
I am the God of the living, not the dead.

I remember
how suddenly I returned to my body,
how I lay quietly in the dark night,
how I thought *Peace. It has covered me,
lifted me up and floated me away.*

I remember
how deeply I slept,
how I woke up to repetition of loved lines.
Was it a vision or a waking dream?
Was it? Did I wake or sleep?

Visitation

Before dawn I felt a touch.
A cold voice whispered *Come*.
A pause. Then that voice again.
Your race you have now run.

I shook my head, withdrew my hand,
weakly whispered *No*.
How can I leave this woman
sitting quietly by the window?

Mr. Death I cannot come!
Look on this vignette—
See how morning's growing light
softly frames her silhouette.

She and I have things to do,
loving not yet completed.
I make this determined vow.
I will not now be defeated.

When you some other time return
I may merely follow,
say goodbye to this
quintessence of joy and sorrow

but now her soft touch makes
your cold grip fall away.
Now I turn again towards light.
Now I again embrace the day.

Recovery

I have been in dark places,
heard Death call my name,
whisper words of promise
to end breath and ease pain.

I have been in clear places,
seen the revelation of light
in the swaying of leaves
so glitteringly bright.

I have been in deep places,
watched in still, joyous trance
bay's water and light play
in sparkling, bright dance.

I have been in loved places,
gained strength to withstand,
felt promise and gained hope
from the soft touch of hand.

I Hear the Music

When these limbs were strong,
when ears were young and clear,
when each day was unblinkingly bright,
much grand music I could not hear.

Now they hear a vast symphony
from stars traversing the night,
and these declining ears hear "alleluia"
from vast pinpricks of cosmic light.

They hear it too from a drop of dew,
hear it from the falling rain,
hear it swell and hear it fade,
hear those motifs return again.

They hear it from a falling leaf,
hear it from the forest floor.
from soaring tree and fallen log
sound melodies that I adore.

They hear it too in baby's cry,
from rosy cheeks and shining hair,
hear from love's deep bond and union
songs with harmonies bright and fair.

They hear this beautiful, symphonic world
filled with the magic of sound.
Hear it swell, rise, crescendo, fall,
echo, harmonise and resound.

They hear it too within my chest,
they hear it from each tiny cell,
hear in the twisted helix of DNA
a great song rise and swell

and though these limbs no longer spring
these fading ears hear the throng
and raising my voice I cry aloud
"I hear the music! I sing the song!"

Into the Wonder

Outside, the eastern rosellas
daily drink at the stone bird bath,
dipping and rising in a flash of colour,
alighting on the leafy branches,
dropping their crimson heads to drink
and then swiftly leaving.
Sometimes black cockatoos
float slowly in lazy flap,
their desolate cry filling the air,
landing to feed on banksia cones
or seeds of the whispering casuarinas.
Sometimes a lone king parrot
briefly visits, flashing feathers
of luminous deep orange
and iridescent green.

Inside, caught in the front door's
ripple of glass, they stay.
The eastern rosella sits on a branch,
always waiting to descend and drink.
A crimson rosella takes flight,
fanning his tail feathers of green and blue.
Another sits quietly, gifting
exquisite crimson, yellow and blue.
Every day they whisper,
"Gaze on us. Let us remind you
of sun and sky, tangle of green,
joy of feather and flight.
Come. Open the door.
Enter into the wonder."

Part 2. A Weight of Thankfulness

The Diamond Python

Under a dome of unrelenting blue
we follow a high plateau
littered with spring flowering,
drop into a gully, cross a creek,
wind our way along the sandstone cliff face,
bend beneath overhangs, squeeze
through narrow gaps between boulders
until finally, there it is, a large shaded rock shelf
overlooking a spectacular network of chasms,
sheer sandstone cliffs sunlit in their ancient weathering,
distant waterfall a wind-blown silver thread,
river unspooling through the green grey scrub,
air full of wind sound and bird song.

We drop our packs, sit in the shade.
We think we have this solitary place to ourselves,
until the owner casually drops in
and pokes his diamond head
through a fissure next to an elbow.
He slithers casually over a backpack,
unhurriedly follows our retreating feet,
unfurling his nine feet of glory.
Large of head, diamond flecked,
he carries the beauty of the night sky
along his thickly muscular length.
He moves from person to person,
slowly traverses the overhang
and then, branch by branch,

with long practised ingenuity
hauls his limbless mass up a tree.

Time passes.
The ancient cliffs grow shadows.
We must retrace our steps,
leave this privileged place
but as we go we carry in our packs
a weight of thankfulness for the diamond Python,
for the gift he has given us,
for his beauty, size, grace and power
and especially for his casual indifference
towards we mere puny humans
now struggling and laboring homewards
through his beauty-filled world.

Seals At Play

Unhindered,
the western waves roll
across three oceans
to crash upon the cliffs.

Unhindered,
southwards the rolling sea
stretches far beyond the horizon
to distant Antarctica.

Unhindered,
the salt-laden wind blows
over the huddling heathland's
wild, remote beauty.

Beneath the cliffs
but above the surge
are crevassed platforms and a curving arch
leading to a pool of mirrored transparency.
Everywhere fur seals bask,
argue over position, laze in the pool
or clamber awkwardly towards the sea.
Where once men clubbed them
to near extinction
they are protected, contented and safe.

Two young seals are at play
in a steep narrow gully,
a rush and retreat

of foaming turbulence and unforgiving rocks.
They surface in tangled somersault,
wrestling, diving, breaching again and again,
young, joyous and unafraid,
toddlers in a playground
confident in their skills,
except this is no playground
or carefully constructed, rubber-layered, safe zone
but the immense, cold, surging,
cliff-pounding sea.

The Eagle

In high, wild wind
I watch her ride corridors of air.
The wind is in her pinions,
in the effortless deftness
and minute calibrations
of her circling glide.
My blurred, distant world
is her sharp focus.
An easy surge corrects her path
and she veers rapidly away
on another current of air.

My voice is a thin whisper
on the high mountainside.
"Queen of air,
hollow-boned,
with dagger talons,
scimitar beak,
gowned in barred brown
and robed in wings more glorious
than garment of embroidered gold,
how you glide, dive and spiral
in majesty and mastery.
Fly close, fix on me
your clear and amber eye,
share with me,
you, who are so high and noble,
so fierce and wild,
so unshackled and free."

Willy Wagtail

Light, agile, acrobatic,
she dances on the fence post,
her gown of black and white
as sleek and smooth
as unruffled satin,
though she owns no other
and wears it day and night.

She fans her little tail.
Her flight is flits and spins,
short jaunts and instant turns,
out, up, down, around,
then back to dance again
on post or strand
of rusting, sagging wire.

Listen to her song.
Chick-a-chick-a-chick.
That is not complaint.
It is celebration.
Listen again.
Now she trills more musically,
her chattering voice
prettily rising and falling
as she pours out into the air only
pure, sweet, bright joy.

Lyre Birds

We walk past the boulder-lined mountain creek,
its tangled profusion of vine and tree,
the spreading glory of the strangler fig
and remnant cedar's towering beauty,

to where in the mountain's slopes
the filtered sun casts a dappled light
and tall trees grow from leaf-littered ground.
There we stop in hushed delight

for two young lyre birds cavort and display,
practising for some more urgent time
their dance, spread of tail and joy of song
with beauty far beyond the power of rhyme.

Their tail is two curves of yellow and black,
enclosing silver gossamer wisp,
as seemingly delicate and coloured
as dew-filled web or wind-blown mist.

This glory they arch over their backs,
graceful, delicate, surprising long,
then dancing a quick, little staccato bob
pour from their throat liquid miracle of song.

From their throat mimicry
in effortless beauty pours-
kookaburra's laugh, whip bird's soar and crack,
king parrot, rosella and many unknown more

and we feel a sense of the sacred
in the ethereal slants of light,
supporting buttress columns of trees,
and this duo praising in unrestrained delight

so we walk hushed from this pure moment
with feelings privileged and sublime,
hearts full of wonder and gratitude,
a sense of a glimpse into the divine,

for on that leaf-littered mountainside
with effortless beauty these small birds raise,
without tuition or much thumbed page,
their wondrous hymn of beauty and praise.

Birds

Its head is brilliant blue,
its composition bright and fair,
and the fairy wren with jaunty flit
hops and bounces through the air.

Its head is pillar-box red,
its flight all speed and swerve
as the rosella glides on brilliant wings
in dipping, parabolic curve.

In his suit of black and white
and rising heavily from the ground,
the magpie flies with a swish
of muscular, purposeful sound.

His song may be a monotonous caw
and his feathers dull and black,
but the crow still rises into the air
in slow, direct and functional flap.

Some pour forth liquid song,
some have plumage bright,
some do flit and some do soar,
some are blessed with speed of flight.

Crow, wren or hawk, I love them all,
and raise my head to stare
in silent praise and wonderment
as they slip and glide in silken air.

i woke this morning

to a neutral voice intoning
bombs in marketplaces
and refugees washed upon the shore

to music of breath and skin
dark cascade of pillowed hair
gossamer feather of touch

to dreams of justice
from the vast sea's edge
to beyond the distant shore

to a jacaranda blue day
dancing through the curtain
and kookaburra's liquid burst of song.

I wake

to the flickering screen's images
of desperation and remorse,
the bleak recounting of misdeeds,
lies, greed, corruption,
scenes of anger, partisan politics, accusation,
analysis, implication, expectation, speculation,
but in the blue-sky day outside
the gum trees are in nectar-filled
explosion of blossom
and the air is filled with flocks
of beautiful rainbow lorikeets
descending to joyously feast
with their excited chatter
and even the grey friar birds,
dipping their dark heads
to fill their curved beaks,
sing their strange chokk-chokk-four-o-clock
in unrestrained, joyous, raucous celebration.

The Phosphorescence Lapping

I raise my eyes
to vast solemnity,
distant fading stars,
great symbols of eternity,

sensing something
veiled from sight,
a portal to reach and tear
and reveal a realm of light,

mysteries
words can never convey,
beyond this time-trapped
confluence of breath and clay,

dimensions
only few have ever seen,
holy men in ages past
in prophecy, vision and dream

but then I know that all
can gaze upon the dew,
the moon upon the water,
the sky's blaze of blue

or in privileged reverence stare
in wonder and in awe
at the phosphorescence lapping
so close upon the shore.

Part 3. Music Everywhere Resounds

Temple

The nave is fields of flowers,
the aisles are snow and forest trees,
the transept is rippling wind on grass,
the altar is the rivers, tides and seas,
the stairwells are mighty mountains
leading to the attic sky
and music everywhere resounds
from wave, bird, storm and soft wind's sigh.
The floating dome is decorated
with ever-changing hue
of billowing white, scudding grey,
or deep ethereal blue,
and fleetingly in east then west
comes a stained-glass blaze of light,
after which the dome transforms
into star-studded velvet night.

Remember

Somewhere there are dark clouds.
Somewhere the oppressor grief adds his heavy weights.
Somewhere there is war, or struggle, or suffering.

But not here.

Here you can see the mild sun
shining in a cloudless sky.
The moving river seems perfectly still,
filled with floating reflections.
A man from long ago
reclines on the sand, a rod in his hand,
although he doesn't care if no fish bite,
and a little fair haired boy, his youngest,
kneels near him laughing in pure childish delight.

Let me fill in some things you cannot see.
To the right is the boulder-filled breakwater
where the river empties into the incessant sea.
To the left a little fleet of trawlers
sit quietly moored to a jetty.
Hidden too, but fixed in memory
and fundamental to the scene,
are his other children, playing in the sand,
laughing and splashing in the shallow water.

Hidden too is the woman, his wife,
who seeing the moment and capturing it, said:

Here. Take this gift and carry it with you.
See what joy is.
Know how it is made of small, inconsequential moments.
Cherish it. Always remember,
no matter what comes or what clouds descend,
this still, blue sky,
lying on this sand, rod in hand,
while the children splash and play.

Wilpena Pound

Lines of low cliff rise abruptly out of arid flatness,
orange in sunlight but purple in shadow.
The scree slopes are dull with stone and desert plant.
There is music here, an uncompromising melody,
abrupt rhythms, discordant tone.
What is the song echoing
through these stern ranges?

Wilpena Pound has a single exit.
A trickle of water feeds a few muddy ponds.
Thickets of huge red gum, artesian fed,
stand sturdily upright or lie tangled
in patterns that momentary torrents of raging water,
briefly and angrily tearing through the gully,
heap along the now near dry river bed.
The music here is countermelody,
lyrical, lush, quiet, secluded,
an interval of contrast before the main theme
insistently and irresistibly sounds from tumbled rock,
thorny desert plants and uncompromising lines of cliff.

I climb to St Mary's Peak.
Southwards stretches the amphitheatre of Wilpena Pound,
enclosed by its vast circle of quartzite walls.
A tenuous scratch of track winds into the Pound.
Northwards the ridged lines of rugged mountains
run in parallel formation to the far horizon,
their boundaries marked, their height and shape fixed
countless millennia before the brief moments

of conquering Alexander or Sennacherib,
or law-maker Moses or wandering Abraham.

I descend, cross the saddle and walk
beneath the orange cliffs.
The air is pure, the wind crisp,
the song of the Flinders clear.
Soon the Evening Star will add its harmony
and later the stars will join in chorus.
The great amphitheatre and its circle of low cliffs
mock pettiness, ambition, vaingloriousness,
but I, a speck in time moving through changelessness,
lift up my eyes to those low cliffs and the towering sky
and hear not defeat or transience or folly
but intimations of the timelessness of eternity.

High Country Rail Trail

From Shelly, now only a green clearing
surrounded by mountain forest,
the meandering descent is gentle.
We pass through a cathedral of trees,
straight, smooth barked and white.
We stop to gaze at yellow-tailed black cockatoos.
Startled deer bound quickly away.
Trestle bridges straddle gullies,
their rustic geometry of heavy timber
now too time worn to safely traverse.
Occasionally a short, shadowed cutting
bludgeons an old path through a low rise.
Lower down, near the undulating valley,
long straight sun-filled causeways
maintain the gradual gradient.
There, in the grasslands,
groups of horses look up and stare
and two young bulls, oblivious to all else,
bellow and shove in dusty, noisy clash.

We meet no-one in all this peaceful day.
Our only companions are shadows:
a surveyor on his horse,
engineers designing their tressels,
groups of labourers sweating and straining
or sitting quietly at smoko while their billy boiled,
farming women travelling home from town.
Gone are the creak then crash of falling trees,
the bush mills cutting timber,

the sound of hammer on steel,
the train smoking over causeway and tressel
and shuddering a slow and winding way
up the steep mountainside.
The stations which once dotted the line
are now only a gash in the scrub.
Time, in a rush of car and truck,
has swept all that work away.
All that remains is the leaf littered track,
the sagging tressels, raised causeway mounds
and a small group of cyclists coasting
easily down the gentle incline alongside
the whispering ghosts of the past.

North of Somewhere

The kilometres slip by as easily as a caress.
You're north of somewhere,
a long, long way from home,
just you and your bicycle
and a tangled profusion of vine and tree
is cascading down the mountain
right to the edge of the sea.

Yesterday's mountains were distant,
green and mottled with sunlight.
Today they are crater lakes;
pelicans gliding in regal stateliness;
a strangler fig like something
out of a fantasy story,
aerial roots descending
in an impenetrable mass of columns
like a monster pipe organ for forest nymphs;
buttress roots twist and turn
in sinuous serpentine curves;
columns of light slant
through the tangled canopy
to the leafy forest floor;
little heritage villages
nestle in wide streets, sprawling corner pubs,
wooden cottages and cool, welcome drinks.

The tyres purr as they touch the road.
The chain whizzes quietly.
Blood pumps through the body.

The mind feels part of something grand.
The spirit fills with the feeling
that every little rise, every corner,
every new day is another adventure,
a magical journey
into the delicious unknown.

La Loire a Velo

We cycle alongside the Loire.
There is birdsong in the air.
We are in no hurry, drifting along
as the Loire makes its full-bodied, green/brown
cloud-shadowed, tree-mirrored, sun-sparkled way
momentarily noisy as it drops over a weir
swirling and eddying around an island
drifting past fields of young, green wheat
burst of new grape leaves
long rows of young corn
bright litter of red poppies
teetering hay-filled barns
villages of cobbled twisting streets
cottage walls bright with roses
grand chateau impregnable on sheer cliff tops
on and on, for hour upon hour
until finally we stop,
tired, glad of rest,
happy to attend to human needs,
to wash, eat, sleep, dream,
while the Loire makes
its full-bodied, green/brown,
cloud-shadowed, tree-mirrored, sun-sparkled way,
swirling, eddying, drifting, meandering

on

      and on

         and on

            and on

At the Victoria & Albert Museum

Two little girls, both about four,
play in the courtyard's shallow pond.
The day is warm. They run and splash
in unselfconscious delight.
I have seen such abandonment before
in a great violinist playing Beethoven's concerto.
I have watched as she was lifted
and then carried away
on the tide of the orchestra.
I saw her surrender to the music,
as if she was a mere instrument
and the orchestra a single entity
chosen for that moment
to transmit wrought transcendence
in all its complex, shifting moods.

The concerto I hear this day is different.
As I watch and listen
I am moved by this question:
in all the marbled stillness inside the museum,
all the carefully re-created rooms,
all the beautiful costumes
from eras long since gone
and all the exquisitely designed rugs
hanging quietly on walls,
is that any greater beauty
than this which I observe
in these two little virtuosos
improvising on their single theme

in a way that requires no rehearsal,
only the abandonment found
in the very young or in great artists,
whilst an orchestra of blue sky, water,
sunlit grass, light on skin and hair,
splash of colour and ripple of laughter
plays in beauty-saturated accompaniment?

Island of Songs

Miranda heard magical music
In percussion crash of wave,
Heard it tinkle in treetop
And echo from distant cave.

Now those same sounds I hear
On this realm of purest sand,
Without pebble, rock, clay or loam,
This beautiful Fraser Island.

It softly and sweetly sings
From serpentine streams so clear
That the mind is forced to question
"Is this water or is this air?"

It murmurs in the mangroves,
The blue of upland lake,
In banksia grove and pandanas plant,
In the forests of coastal she-oak.

It crescendos in the rainforest's
Green palms that densely entwine,
Its soaring white towers of blackbutt,
Its spotted beauty of Kauri pine.

It sounds from eastern waves
That daily wash from their sand
The countless tracks of the 4 wheel drives
That scurry upon the land.

And even though on the morrow
That traffic will again resume,
Closely following the tide will sing
Its lyrical, relentless cleansing tune.

O gently, gently each day
The attendant tide comes in
And with song of ease and grace
Makes everything pristine again.

Then the magic that Miranda heard
Ripples or crashes in the sea,
Or in the high, bright notes of the treetops
Makes songs of exquisite beauty.

Evening

places diamonds in the blue-black sky,
clothes the horizon in orange glow,
the sea in silver shimmer
and the distant clouds in purple gown.

Even the houses on the low hills
transform into sparkles of coloured light
and all the land's imperfections, pock marks and wrinkles
brush clean away by her gentle touch.

The Fallen Forest Tree

I think on this blue planet,
slant of rain, scud of cloud,
surge of river, the glittering sea,
flocks that flit, dart or soar,
wandering herds, encircling wolves,
coral blaze, fish, whale and krill,
leopard lazing in curve of tree,
myriad life given and accepted back
over aeons as the spinning earth treks
through the black void of space.

I raise my eyes from the fallen tree
to the treetops and to the sky.
The abundant cycle of life and loss
stretches endlessly beyond
this transient moment where I live,
yet why should I regret its brevity?
I embrace its mystery and privilege,
thankful that for at least this brief moment
I have lived to gaze upon the earth
in deep wonder and in awe.

Desert Ruin

Trees huddle in dry, rocky creek beds.
Beyond the horizon's heat-haze
the distant mirage shimmers
and the Flinders Ranges
rise suddenly in knuckled lumps.

In the stark beauty
of this barren world
a single ruin crumbles,
a doorway and a few walls
all that remain of a dream
that sparkled, sweated,
flickered and died.

Then, beneath the dome
of cloudless blue
or star-littered black,
the flat land shrugged off
the puny human scratches
and returned to its harsh eternity.

Spring

I give thanks for this spring day,
this blue-sky, cloud-scudded, leaf-swaying day,
this glistening, sparkling, sun-filled day,
this dappled, shade-strewn, patterned day,
this magnolia-blooming, freesia-littered, plum-blossoming day,
this bud-swelling, bird-singing, spring-cool fresh day,
this day that turns its back on winter's cold,
this day of growth, colour and warmth,
this day of birth and laughter and song,
this tender day, this day of beginnings,
this lung filling, mind uplifting, joyous day,
this day when the heart swells and hope, like sap, rises,
this day when the world seems bright and light-
yes, I give thanks for the glory of this day.

Summer Inferno

The familiar blue sky has disappeared.
Through smoke haze the sun rises and sets flouro pink.
The drought ridden, heat saturated, continent blazes.
The temperature rises to 48C.
We venture into its sledgehammer blow
to fill up the sandstone birdbaths.
Hundreds of birds congregate around the precious water.
There is no profligate splashing.
The friar birds dip their slender, curved beaks,
rise to swallow, then dip again.
From the gleditsia's pendant branches
hundreds of rainbow lorikeets
drop to the precious water in iridescent flutter.

I think of those estimates of 500 million animals lost.
I see again the woman rushing through a firey landscape,
ripping off her shirt and wrapping it around a burnt koala.
Someone posts a video of hundreds of kangaroos
going hard up a smoke-filled hill.
There are challenging images of horses and cattle
lying prone in burnt out paddocks,
behind them a backdrop of blackened trees.

The trees grow thickly and are burning.
A fire truck moves along a fire trail.
Someone says, *Better get that fire blanket up, mate*
but as they fumble the trees erupt,
an ember storm envelops them and flames
leap thirty metres above the trees and rush at the road.

Keep going, Bob, the same voice says,
his voice filled with tension and encouragement.

The word comes to the little coastal holiday towns.
It's too late to pack up and go.
There is only one road in and they
are hemmed in by spotted gum forest.
In surreal night-in-day light,
holidayers and locals huddle together on the beach.
Fire rages to the dunes, leaping and roaring,
crowning high above the tree tops.
Even the grasses on the low dunes burn.
There is an audible gasp as a house explodes.
A helicopter dumps a load of water on it
but there is no diminishment of flame.

Flames are everywhere. It seems as if these scenes
have been filmed through a deep red filter.
At midday it is as dark as night,
blackness surreally saturated in red.
The wind is howling and the sea surges and swells.
A man, a tough guy used to hardship,
flees with his family in his boat.
He wears goggles and a mask.
His voice is usually the flat intonation of one
used to hiding his feelings.
Now it bristles with unadorned emotion.
The fire front's just come through. Faarrk.
I hope everyone's just farking…Faarrk…Fark the houses man.
Get into the water. It's farking chaos.

Watching those scenes of apocalypse,
I can't not think of the post inferno chaos

and what will we leave for future generations.
Seven billion humans inhabit and share
with other life this finite blue planet.
Is it possible to find a way to live on it and with it,
or will humans, following visionless leaders,
continue to grope a blind, indulgent way,
squabbling, scapegoating and consuming
until nothing is left but warring remnants
locked in ferocious conflict over the charred remains.

Autumn Day

In this part of her southern kingdom
she slips in quietly, pre-dawn,
opening windows,
letting the heat of summer seep away.
A thin mist hovers briefly on the river,
then lifts into the still sky.
On the mirrored surface
the smooth, white trunked water gums
hang upside down in sky
blue from horizon to horizon.
The day shortens.
Westwards, the distant mountains,
blue by day, darken to purple.
Above them, briefly,
a swathe of orange.
Above that the indigo sky
and the Evening Star.
Then the orange dims
and black, velvet night,
diamond studded, descends
over the quiet and cooling earth.

Winter

See how
on this rainy day
the banksias dress
in burnished gold

and how
on frosty mornings
the humble wattle displays
her summery-yellow sprays

or how
through the gloom
of grey cloud's cluster
the sun pokes his bright toe

and hope that,
in whatever darkness,
come splashes of yellow and gold
and descending columns of light.

Home

The butcher bird pours
liquid ripple of song
into the blue sky.

The rosella dips his red head
at the stone bird-bath
and drinks in alert delight.

We sit on the verandah.
Your eyes smile.
I reach for your hand.

Part 4. Melody Upon Melody

My Flawed Love

Morning light is filled with gold
Of delicate, transient hue;
The noonday sky is beautiful
With its deep and ethereal blue;
The momentary grandeur in the west
Is repeated transforming delight,
Followed by that changing mystery,
The silken lustre of the night.
O they can boast of their display
But I will count our love more rare:
Say they have no voice to speak, no lips to kiss,
No minds to knit, no hands to care,
And in repetition they come then fade away,
Whilst my flawed love grows with each passing day.

Earth Music

An intricate, richly sensual tune
this tactile, perfumed earth sings
and to the song of sun, sea and moon
all creation its own harmony brings.
The lover sun holds earth in his arms,
the insatiable sea caresses the shore,
the night is besotted by the moon's charms
and everywhere is the cry for more.
Flowers willingly open for honey bees,
clouds are the vaporous water's embrace,
and with earth and sea the insistent breeze
communes as if face to face.

Thus every creature is entranced
by the music that around them flows
and caught up in this harmony dance
patterns each intuitively knows.
All these are creatures of the dust
caught in earth's scent and song,
singing and dancing in the way they must
patterns of desire to which they belong.
Whether in stealth, danger or death,
in grace, beauty or fluttering need,
in savagery or urgent stress,
all play in earth's rich symphony of seed.

So you and I, who smell the perfumed air,
are caught and enfolded by this song
and to its great pattern and desire

our lives in close union belong.
The sounds ringing with rich complexity
melody upon melody entwine,
and tenderness, love and fidelity
in its high, clear, pure notes shine.
O my love, I in this great world stand
surrounded by rich music of life,
sustained in spirit, heart, mind and hand
by you – my partner, my joy, my wife.

River

The current sweeps us along,
past laugh and splash of free running water,
over falls that shout and plunge,
alongside the red poppy fields,
under green pendant willows,
around curving bends and lazy meander
towards, in the distance,
the still dark sea.

Long ago there was a morning
filled with sunshine and bird song.
Somehow, wonderfully, you passed by.
I reached out, felt your hand and it closed on mine.
Why? The body's desire?
The mind's fear of loneliness?
A beauty of need, to love and be loved?
Who can know, but every day
sunlight caressed the waves
and every night the current filled
with silken sheen from moon and star.

We are closer now to the rumbling confluence
where river protests to meet the sea.
Does that matter?
Long ago our deep union consumed me,
took me way out
beyond sheltered cove or stagnant stillness,
deep, deep into a trackless wonder,
into mighty waves of beauty and joy,

deep troughs of compassion
for heartache and pain,
a pure, sublime tide far beyond self.

There I have richly dwelt.
There, in wonder and surrender,
I have willingly sunk and drowned.

This Passing Day

It seems to me that the brittle-bright morning
when we first loved
was a glistening shimmer of dew drop.
All the world's wealth was ours.
Time seemed held in fragile crystal stop.

Now it is late afternoon.
The sky is clear and the sinking sun
more intensely beautiful than it was long ago.
Who can know if night will suddenly fall
or day stretch on past midnight
in muted, dimming, surreal twilight.

No matter. Each transient moment is rich with joy
and passing time has been our strange friend,
gifting us a plaited golden cord that twists and entwines,
tying us to each other and to the present,
the past and the unknowable future.

So come, take my hand.
That fragile morning is long gone.
Evening must fall but the stars promise light.
We have lived and loved together,
shared in glory throughout the long passing day.
Is this not enough?
It must be enough.

It is much more than enough.

I know

you are a gift from God
and you were wondrous fair:
your lovely eyes,
your tender lips,
your silken cascade of coal black hair.

To your soft touch the waves lap close
then tumble over my head.
In ecstatic joy
and deep embrace
you take me to your bed.

My greatest joy is beyond compare,
the cord which does most bind:
the relentless chime
of tangled time
ties me in unity to your mind.

Years have passed and lips do fade
but love has wondrously grown:
more dear to me,
still marvelously,
my gift from God alone.

Come, Hold Me

Come, hold me,
for the world is so mingle mixed,
so contrastingly, proportionally fixed-
pain flooded, beauty buoyant,
achingly sad, fleetingly joyous,
poignantly littered, pathos strewn,
touchingly tender, savagely hewn-
for under this blue, beauty-laden sky
we laugh, labor, mourn and sigh,
seek answers to an unknowable why,
see much to make the tender heart cry-
so hold me. Make all seem bright.
Tenderly grant me your sweet respite.
Bathe me in your wonder and light.
Momentarily wash away the night.

Fate

Dad never spoke about the war,
although, in hindsight,
its heavy hand was everywhere.
Maybe Mum told me the fragment,
the amazing flying away part.
The rest is in my mind.

First, I see the night,
then the twin-engined Vickers Wellington
taking off from Gibraltar and flying out
over the approaches to the Mediterranean.
I see six young men,
all brave, dutiful, all with a sense of honor,
but all of whom have seen loss,
been shocked by it and become resigned to it.
Each evening they fly out into uncertainty.
I am not yet born but one of them I know well.
I have often seen his young face in photos.
I know he is 12,000 kms from home.
I know his little country town, the green valley,
the temperamental river.
I know those who live there,
his mother and father, his brothers and sister,
his young wife and the child he has never seen.

The night passes.
The first light is in the sky.
The silver-grey sea barely ripples beneath them.
The Rolls Royce engines drone.

They have seen nothing.
All is routine. They must head back to base.
Their lumbering plane is vulnerable in the daylight.
Then someone stares and squints.

Bloody hell, what's that block dot?
I think it's a fighter.
Ours or theirs?
O God, it's a Messerschmitt.
He's seen us, boys. He's heading straight for us.
He's too bloody fast. He'll catch us.
Get ready, boys. Give him hell.

The tail gunner and nose gunner
swivel their guns.
The Radio Operator, the one I know well,
rushes to an extra gun.
I hear their thoughts.

We'll never outrun him.
There's cannons in his wings.
We've only got machine guns.
One of us might get lucky.
Concentrate. Concentrate. Aim.
Give it your best.

Suddenly, almost within range,
the Messerschmitt turns and flies parallel to them.
He tips his wings, back and forth, back and forth,
a kind of greeting, an acknowledgement
before he peels off and flies away.
They watch him receding,
become a black dot and then disappear.

A wave of relief rushes over them.
They are incredulous.
A crazed kind of laughter echoes through the plane.
They will drink when they land.

But in the Messerschmitt that flies away
sits a young man tired of war,
tired of killing, tired of the mad folly of it.
He knows that plane, its vulnerabilities, its blind spots.
He knows he could have fired his cannons
through its canvas and into the flesh of the men inside,
or into the engines and he knows
he could have watched
their slow, smoke-filled spiral into the water below.
He has seen too much of war and death.
He is past inflicting harm or even wishing it.
Are not those men his brothers?
What difference is there but place of birth?

And he knows, too,
with a sad but wished-for resignation,
that his time will come soon, soon.
He has heard his engines scream,
seen his billowing smoke,
seen the water rushing up to meet him.
He will kill no more and someone, somewhere,
a mother or lover, will shed tears for him.

And the man in the Wellington,
one of the six, the one I know well,
is free to head back to the rocky little island,
free to fly again, free to go into his future,
free to embrace his yet to be known,

his great tangled twist of life and fate,
his triumphs and struggles,
his laughter, joy and pain.
He is free to one day return
to the life he left,
to his wife and child
and to four more unborn children
still waiting somewhere in the future's silence.

The Millet Cutters

First light streaks pastel pink.
Mist floats on the river.
Cattle stand quietly
under bamboo clumps.
A willy wagtail flicks and fidgets
on a strand of barbed wire.
Millet grows in neat rows,
tall and straight, ready for harvest.
Five men gather around their utes,
cane cutters in the off-season.

Laughter. Hard men,
status wrought from endurance.
In the early light we move
backwards through the rows,
then the glint of sharp knives,
chug of tractor, the trailer filling,
sweat, heat, smoko, hot black tea,
color in the western sky,
and the tired, slow walk at day's end.

Those men are long gone.
Time took their bodies
and machines their work,
but I see the fields in harvest,
the quiet men gathered
at the long day's end,
Bull Williams, needing to be fastest,

Carusi with his broken English
dreaming of his own farm
and gentle, generous Mike,
who'd fought at Milne Bay,
now backlit by the fading light
as he moves through the rows
with long, easy strides
towards his waiting ute.

I Am Amongst the Richest of Men

There once was a time when I was poor,
when my house was dim and empty,
when wind rattled through my empty vaults
with a bleak insistent constancy.

But I am amongst the richest of men,
my vault has wealth untold,
my treasury is full of sparkling things
and I dwell in a palace of gold.

My wealth is based on four unique pillars,
from one quarry cut but standing discretely,
and now I declare that I love each one
completely, fervently and equally.

Did I once fear that this wealth must leave
and the cold, empty wind could blow again?
No! Time has wrought the hoped-for change;
this wealth — my children — have become my friends.

For my wealth is not in things that rust,
or moth can corrupt, or thief can steal,
for I am rich in care, hope and love,
in all the deep things the heart can feel.

So I value but little success or fame,
or any of the trinkets for which men lust.
Compared to the things in which I am rich
they are not much more than worthless dust.

So I am amongst the richest of men,
my vault has wealth untold,
my treasury is full of sparkling things
and I dwell in a palace of gold.

Hush

Hush, tread quietly and don't disturb
for here is a moment to always treasure.
Eleanor Miette, though she's less than one
is looking at books and chatting with pleasure.

Hush, tread quietly and softly retreat,
tiptoe so gently from this place.
Who for a moment would ever disturb
the look of pure joy all over her face.

Hush, tread quietly and don't disturb,
yet linger a moment for one last little look,
for this little girl, though she's less than one
is lost in the world of a wonderful book.

Mother and Child at Piano

Light spills through the room
where Prue sits at piano,
Eleanor on lap.

As the fingers touch
in light skillful patterns
chords fluidly flow.

The sweet sound is as
liquid, clear and delicate
as running water.

The baby gurgles
her new, innocent delight
and waves her little arms,

Bella

She kneels
amongst the strawberries,
sunshine in her hair.

"I can do it Pa."
Her little hand takes the plant
and parts the rich earth.

She snuggles in close.
Her arms encircle my neck.
I feel her eyes shine.

Ten thousand thousand
small, miraculous moments
fill my heart with joy.

.

At Piano

She keeps her sadness hidden,
eyes clear and direct,
mouth curved in a gentle smile,

but when her hands touch the keys,
a new richness seeps
through her fingers, hangs

for a trembling moment
in the expectant air,
then disperses into our changed minds.

Part 5. The Tide Rushes Out

Lament for a Light Horseman

How young and dashing you are.
You wear your emu-plumed Light Horseman's hat.
Your face, in profile, is full of hope.
A little smile flickers on your lips.
Bright confidence covers your face.
You hold her by the bridle throatlatch.
Her mixture of fear and curiosity amuses you.
Her ears are forward. Her eyes stare.
What is it that you whisper?
Don't worry, Pol, it's only a camera.
Click! And there you are, for that moment
always young, happy and idealistic.
Perhaps you were just twenty-two.

That was before your marriage,
before you left for war,
before you left behind your pregnant wife,
before, night after night, 17,000 kilometers from home
you spent the years of what remained
of your young life in the danger and cold
of a canvas-covered aircraft,
protecting Allied shipping lanes,
searching for U-boats,
skimming low over the blue Mediterranean
and then later the dark, cold North Sea,
unwaveringly following your conscience,
surviving who knows what
to finally come home.
Then you were just thirty-three.

I wish I could write a happy ending for you,
one like those Westerns you so loved,
have your horse, Polybon, waiting for you,
have you hero-like swing into the saddle,
lift your bride up behind you,
and whilst the credits roll
turn away from the camera and canter
towards family and contentment
in those distant blue mountains.
But that is not your story.
After eighteen happy and generous years
when your family grew and you rebuilt your life,
you became sick, your lungs shrunk,
your evenings were destroyed with coughing
and a desperate struggle for air.
You said it was chronic illness from the War.
You said it was from flying in the freezing night.
Eventually a reluctant government agreed.
You were only fifty-one.

If I could, I would wash away
those last seventeen years,
when something dark and terrible
and utterly beyond your control
emerged to periodically overpower
who I think you wanted to be.
I would fetch from a deep well
water of such sweetness
as to soothe and heal all your mind's wounds.
What would have made you happy?
I have seen in that portrait
the young man you once were
and the person you wanted to be.

Now, if I could, I would tell you
that these older eyes have searched your deep core
and found a complex and good man trapped
by something vastly beyond his control.

You did not live a long life.
Your heart gave out.
We gathered around you in the hospital,
your wife and four of your five children.
For more than a week you lingered,
gaining comfort from our presence.
Then you fell into unconsciousness
and the green monitor flat-lined.
He's gone, I said.
He's not, she said, in momentary disbelief.
Then briefly and tenderly she touched you,
forehead to forehead, before,
emotionally exhausted, we left together
in strange mixture of grief and relief.
You were not quite sixty-eight.

Homecoming

We pause for a quiet moment
beside the weatherboard house
that she lived in as a girl.
She carries a small plastic bag.
We walk beside a narrow path
and descend on steps cut into a steep bank.
Mum used to maintain these, she says.
They were only dirt then.

At the bottom is a stony beach
and the Derwent, hundreds of meters wide.
I built a little safe pool out of rocks for Susan here.
She loved it so much.
She always cried when we left.
Mum could hear us returning.

A brief, complex blend of emotions suddenly rush in,
joy and love, a sense of pride that I know her,
that I have lived my adult life with her,
but loss too, a regretful sense of passing time.
I see her as a girl, slender, dark haired,
carrying her baby sister home
up the steep bank to their waiting mother,
or playing on these rocks, naming them,
laughing with childish delight,
plunging into the cold water.

She points to two of the larger rocks.
That one is Biggie. That's Flattie.

She takes off her shoes, walks to Flattie,
kneels, undoes the plastic bag
and empties a little into the water.
The wind catches the finer particles.
She pauses then empties the rest.
A cloud appears in the water and briefly spreads.
The waves come in again, slap on the rock and suck back.
The cloud spreads a little more and then it is gone.
This great earth, giver and nurturer of life,
absorbs the remains of one who lived so passionately,
loved so fiercely, whose beauty was a light,
who was uncompromisingly upright,
who, like all who tread the earth,
had strengths and weaknesses, triumphs and losses
but who loved and was loved in return.
Earth and wind and water now have her.
She is at one with countless billions
whose life has been given and taken back.

We hug briefly. No need for words.
We climb the earthen steps.
At the top blackberries grow wild.
They carry both flowers and fruit.
Most of the fruit is red but some are black.
We pick a few and taste them.
They're still a bit bitter, she says,
as we turn and walk slowly away.

Summers With Jean

For fifty summers I went to Jean.
The dunes between her house and the sea
were wild and thick with banksia and honey eaters.
To the right a kilometer away the little fishing village
was unchanging except for gathering dust-
breakwater, river, fleet of trawlers,
and Johnny's milk bar.
To the left the crescent beach curved away
into the distant horizon,
just waves and sand and a fisherman
standing shin deep in the ebb and flow.

Waves crash. The tide moves.
The ebb and flow of fifty summers comes and goes.
Here a little boy plays in the sand.
Here he rows on the river with his bride.
Here his children laugh and splash.
Somewhere, dim and vague,
beyond his memory, wrapped in mist,
Jean loses her only child
and Clive, her husband, dies,
but clear in memory,
in inconsequential things,
here and here and here and here
she triumphs in generosity, humor,
energy, indomitable spirit and love.

Still the insistent waves roar and crash.
The tide rushes out, too far, too fast.

Children grow.
Jean grew old.
Then frail.
Then she died.

There is no going back,
though waves still crash on the sand
and solitary fishermen still stand knee deep in the waves.
Some things are too changed for returning
except, in cherished memory,
where I always see her in her garden,
sit with her in the cool of the afternoon,
and hear, with her,
the eternal sound of the sea
thumping on the sand
and then, slowly,

its long,

aching,

melancholy

withdrawal.

Elegy for Ikeogu Oke

Always the relentless tide comes in.
Sometimes it snatches a child.
Sometimes an adolescent is held in its suck.
Sometimes it takes the infirm
waiting silently on the beach in hope of release.
Always it sucks back, carrying them out
into the vast, dark wasteland,
a region beyond the sight of the living
who play in the sun in the knowledge
that one day a wave will roll in for them.

Sometimes it comes for one such as you,
someone in the prime of life,
someone garlanded with deserved honours,
someone with a wife and young children,
someone with a mind clear and deep
and crackling with ideas
and in whom adversity and courage
had forged a character bold, truthful
and uncompromisingly upright.

Then our tears must flow.
Our hearts must mourn.
In our spirit we groan and sigh.
We wear the heavy mantle grief.
We stand and gaze out to sea.
But we cannot seek there forever.
The living will return to life,
to joy, to celebration, to love,

to songs celebrating our brief moments
in the wonder of the world.

In my song of living I will make praise for you.
I will celebrate that I have known you.
I will rejoice in your life.
I will rejoice in *The Heresaid*,
your masterwork that for years
you honed and polished into perfection
with no knowledge of the honours it would bring.
I will rejoice that our minds met
and our friendship flourished.

You have gone and yet you still are with us.
You have not drifted anonymously away.
You have touched hearts.
You will touch hearts yet to be born.
Your legacy is not just your work.
You have left a reminder of what
we flawed humans can be.
I want to take your diligence, your honesty,
your uncompromising adherence
to the search for truth,
your generosity,
your belief in justice and equity,
your love of creative endeavour
and your ceaseless search for its perfection,
yes, take them and desire that they live in me
as a continual reminder of you,
you, who it was my privilege to know,
you, who I celebrate,
you, who I praise,
you, whose name I say,

Ikeogu Oke,
great poet,
clear thinker,
wonderful man,
dear friend,
now gone
too young.

Somme Cemetery

A soft grey mist covers the distant ridges,
lies close upon the green folds
and drips off the thousands of white crosses
standing rigidly at parade ground attention,
marked with this sad simplicity:
"A Soldier of the Great War".

Hard to think that in this landscape a century ago
a nightmarish Nationalism
opened its maw and rumbled creaking
over the green folds, quiet woods and farmlands,
venting a reeking stench
of mud, barbed wire, crater holes, shells, gas,
kilometer upon winding kilometer of trenches
and a tangled twist of young lives
stuck in the mud or huddled
beneath the thud of artillery
or emerging into the staccato spray of machine gun.

Yes, it is quiet. The landscape is green.
The guns have gone. The young men are dust.
Gone too are their mothers, or lovers,
their brothers, sisters, family, friends.
Gone too is the mud, the gas, the trenches,
the inconsolable grief and loss,
but a soft grey mist covers the distant ridges,
lies close upon the green folds
and drips off the thousands of white crosses

marked with this sad simplicity:
"A Soldier of the Great War"—

For the day is weeping, quietly weeping,
and must go on weeping still.

Koko and the Beast

This week, two stories.
One beautiful, sad, heart-rending.
The other?
Make up your own mind.

In one story an inflated emptiness
struts and preens in hollow vanity,
boasting of wealth and power
as his mirror audience
claps and cheers and chants

whilst the world fills with tears
from children of the poor,
hiding under space blankets,
their crying for their mothers

rising high above the clamour,
the lies and self-justifications,
the heartless mis-use of law and Bible,
the faux "I'm a mother and a catholic" outrage.

In the other story Koko,
the western lowland gorilla,
dies peacefully,
aged forty six.

Intelligent Koko,
who could sign 1000 words
and understand 2000.

Gentle Koko,
who, tired and near the end,
signed to her friend
"I'm getting old".

Loving Koko,
who, though childless,
raised two kittens
and thought of them as hers.

Mourned Koko,
missed by Ndume,
who, arranging blankets around her body,
signed "I know" and "Cry".

Koko,
let me also mourn for you.
Let me praise you too.
Strange consolation
to know of life such as yours,
intelligent, simple and pure,
utterly without vanity,
a light in the darkness
of all the coiffed, self-serving horror
now strutting the stage of the world
and beating at the hollow chest
of its own vast emptiness.

The Green Sea Turtle

Is she gliding or soaring?
Each beat of her wing-like flippers
propels her massive weight
with its gleaming black carapace
through the trackless ocean
with movement as graceful as flight.

Something beyond reason
guides her a thousand kilometres
to the sandy island of her birth,
to waiting males, mating,
labouring up the beach,
laying her clutch of eggs,
then dragging her great weight back
into the buoyancy of the sea.

Will she one year make her journey in vain?
Will male green turtles no longer
glide through the water near her island?
Is the incubating sand growing too warm?
Will then only females hatch
to run the gauntlet of crab, bird or dog
before they reach the swell
and the empty refuge of the sea?

Advertisement

For Sale.
Planet Earth,
The Solar System,
Orion Arm,
The Milky Way.

This planet,
filled with abundant life
and suggestion of spirit-force,
is slightly used
but has great potential.

Prospective buyers will notice
some wear at the Poles,
difficulty with the air-conditioning,
considerable habitat loss,
coral bleaching,
and species extinction
due to short-term thinking
from the dominant species.

Repairable with care and planning,
the site retains much natural beauty.
In particular, the dome
remains largely untouched,
ethereal blue by day,
stained-glass beauty
morning and evening,
diamond-studded velvet quilt at night.

Other features include
snow capped mountains,
vast oceans that crash on cliffs
or curl and slap on sand,
rivers that rush, fall, roar, meander,
and a dazzling array of vegetation
too varied to list.

But hurry.
A myopic beast called "Corporation",
caring little for plunder and greatly for profit,
is intent on consuming everything in the yard.

All responsible buyers are welcome.
Please organize inter-galactic
visiting rights before inspection.

Interim Report

Unseen, we hovered above the planet.
It has retained much of its beauty:
grassed plains, high mountains, sky and cloud,
spectacular displays from land and sea.

However, we noted damage and scarring.
Floating islands of plastic and huge holes abound.
Grey smudges and stagnant water indicate
considerable pollution of air, water and ground.

We also noted the dominant species
has a limited, self-centred thinking.
Inequality and poverty are rife.
Egalitarian ideals appear to be shrinking.

Problems demand altered consciousness.
Poverty, resource plundering, increasing population,
primitive energy sources and climate warming
indicate a need for global cooperation.

Most of the wealth is controlled by a few.
To protect it they exploit a common flaw
which enables many to be easily manipulated
into the absurdity of destruction and war.

We believe they slumber in partial consciousness.
They are not yet fully awake.
Further development may require
an emotional and intellectual earthquake.

We will return in a millennium or two.
The species has potential for distinction.
We conclude with the hope that their folly
does not ultimately lead to their extinction.

Can We Not Live Together?

I gave you all, said,
"Come, lie with me,
gaze on me, caress me.
I give you life and beauty too-
all I have is yours to share
but please place me gently in your care."

But you have torn my garments,
scarred my face, besmirched my skin,
gouged my secret parts-
your rule, cruel; your treatment, rough;
so insatiable you can never get enough.

I writhe in protest.
I heave and crack.
I send mighty tempests.
I stop the rain.
I send parching heat.
I struggle and strive.
I cry out for help.
I say,

"Come, repent, be my friend,
be tender, gentle, make amends.
It is not yet too late to start again.
Think of the future,
before the children bemoan your folly,
curse your abusive misrule,
and you for being a short-sighted fool."

O can we not live together?
I give you life and beauty too.
Can you then not care for me,
love me, work with me
or must I, at last, finally, regretfully,
in deepest sorrow
turn my back and put you out?

Then

Then the earth went quiet.
No creature called.
No background hum.
No crickets, cicadas, frogs.
Birds gasped, opened their beaks,
held out their wings to cool,
then fell to the ground.

Then water took low atolls,
covered dunes,
inched up river valleys,
covered abandoned houses
and twisted war machines,
lapped tall towers
still standing like strange sentinels
in the orange tinted tide.

Then, on the far horizon,
the sun flamed dirty smudge,
lit the mountains
and the haggard faces
of the survivors
moving higher and higher
over the pock-marked land.

Then suddenly it dipped
into impenetrable black.
No silver pepper of stars.

No moon, though the ocean
still ebbed and flowed.
Then only darkness
covered the face
of the mighty deep.

The Gathering Host

Australia's jewel is burning.
All along the rugged, mountainous south-west coast
of the island state of Tasmania,
rain-forests, once a tangle of towering trees and vine,
stand dry and vulnerable.
The host has ceased its gathering.
Now it attacks with a roar.
It overpowers the King Billy pines.
It plunders alpine garden and rainforest.
It gathers to scale the Walls of Jerusalem.
Its front line stretches for 1600 kilometres.
What stops it turning towards the populated east,
raging through farmland and city,
burning down to the water
before jumping channels to conquer the islands,
the sapphire splints off the mainland gem?
Only the wind which refuses to blow.
But still, it smoulders in the deep gorges
and blazes through button grass and rainforest.

Northwards, over the vast continent,
the land bakes under 40 C heat.
The Darling River runs dry.
Where only algae blooms in oxygen-deprived ponds,
a million fish lie belly up and stinking.
Starving roos die of thirst.
Koalas leave the trees in search of moisture.
The land pants and cracks and subsides.
The fear of summer spreads

as heat wave follows heatwave,
blanketing the inland,
surging over the Great Dividing Range,
oppressing the white sand beaches
and the curling blue waves.

Still fools wave lumps of coal in Parliament.
Still powerful politicians live in denial.
Still the hollow men
stuff their headpiece filled with straw
into their dry cellar.
And I ask this.
Is this the way the world ends?
Is this the way the world ends?
Is this the way the world ends?
Not with a bang.
Nor with a whimper.
But with a mighty conflagration?

It's Not Our Fault

A million fish lie white-belly up and rotting
in shallow water of the Darling River.
The mighty river with its 40,000 year old fish traps
is drying into a dying trickle,
its tributaries into muddy ponds.
Upstream, corporate cotton growers
squint and stare over vast irrigation reserves.
"It's not our fault," they say.
"We only take our entitlement.
It's the drought. Blame nature."
Downstream, the pumps with their
too often deregulated water metres
steal the precious scarce water
into networks of open channels.
It's not our fault," they say.
"Everybody's doing it.
It's the drought. Blame nature."
Across the entire basin and beyond,
nearly half the Australian continent,
a record heatwave looms.
Summer temperatures soar to 47C.
Plants droop. Water holes are mud.
Panting roos seek relief but find none.
Birds sit noiseless and still, wings and beaks open.
"It's a tragedy," says the politician,
"But it's not our fault.
There's not much we can do.
It's the drought. Blame nature."
But a million fish lie white-belly up and stinking

in the algae bloom oxygen-deprived water
and each day come warnings
of more disaster to come.

The Plum Tree

For my grandchildren.

Look little ones,
the leaves have turned yellow,
the sky is pure blue,
the day mild and mellow.

Look little ones,
the tree is now bare,
there's frost in the morning
and cold everywhere.

Look little ones,
there's buds on the trees,
flowers are blossoming
and buzzing with bees.

Look little ones,
in this blossoming blooming
the cycle of life
is forever renewing.